Trilogy

Doreen Gildroy

New Issues Poetry & Prose

A Green Rose Book

New Issues Poetry & Prose
The College of Arts and Sciences
Western Michigan University
Kalamazoo, Michigan 49008

Printed in the United States of America.

First Edition, 2018.

ISBN: 978-1-936970-52-0 (paperbound)

Library of Congress Cataloging-in-Publication Data:
Gildroy, Doreen
Trilogy/Doreen Gildroy
Library of Congress Control Number: 2017919167

Editor:	William Olsen
Managing Editor:	Kimberly Kolbe
Layout Editor:	Danielle Isaiah
Art Direction:	Nicholas Kuder
Design:	Matthew Poleo
Production:	Paul Sizer
	The Design Center, Frostic School of Art
	College of Fine Arts
	Western Michigan University
Printing:	McNaughton & Gunn, Inc.

Trilogy

Doreen Gildroy

New Issues
WESTERN MICHIGAN UNIVERSITY

Also by Doreen Gildroy

The Little Field of Self
Human Love

for Emily

and for Michael

Contents

Celestial Room

Uncreated Light

Labyrinth On My Table

Celestial Room

I will first spend a great deal of time in seeking Happiness, and then a Great deal more in Enjoying it....I will now spend Days and Nights in Possessing it. as I did before in seeking it. It is better being Happy, then Asleep.

—Thomas Traherne, *Centuries*

In The Bed

At the children's hospital entrance,
carrying her over the bricks, incessant—

with the names of the dead ones
burned into them—

my husband says
Your whole world breaks open.

Lying in the open bed with her—
so she would not fall.

We move through time together.

How many days has it been?

And the other babies crying.

*

How one is struck. How another.
I cannot easily conclude.

In her cry

everything moved before me—
color and shade,
in the evening sky.

I could only feel *preciousness*—

(though I could think many things).

*

Was I worthy? Lovely?:

they are torments.
I was never free

to see myself
limited and alive.

No matter what we have to go through, he said.

And in my solemnity
I offer
only

what I am.

*

Sometimes I like that light

the hour
when Doctor Greene comes in—

and we will speak
about her.

I can't worry about my life:

it is a glimpse, a refraction of light.

*

Not just her suffering draws me near:
it is unblemished—
with a forceful face

toward the direction of the sun:

she likes that light
coming through the slate-grey blinds
which must be—to her—
geometric shape.

*

Child of morphine, child of pain.
Placing the salve upon her face

in disbelief that I am doing it.
From my hands.

I had imagined everything was separate
and together.
I imagined a beautiful creature
and I held to that image.

The catheter in,
the bandages off.

It was good to go to sleep.
It was clean.

The House I Am In

Not dead
(in concealment)
                                        dead to the world
                                        dead to the light

I was going forward—
shrouded
in the quiet
even to myself

(I am the person
I have lived)—
Her face buried in my arms,
and we go forth.

Looking At The Fountain In The Sun

If this really were just a *dead place*
how could it feel
so *uncoverable*?

I began to understand
uttermost, unspeakable—
and what was at the midpoint?

We were holding hands,
and walking
and she became very quiet and
still
before the fountain.

Which was the feeling
that was the real feeling?
The true one
(the self)
innermost and resting?

And which was the living that would
sprout up—
a little green?

The Solitary Darkness

It was a clear thing, a clear picture;

it was a place that could
waver.

When the elders came
to speak to me—

to assess me—

I would want to answer

(could all my voices all be true?)
when I felt only the *must I*?

*

Light and shadow:
this is where we belong.

I was looking forward to spring, the sun.
It was like being in a cell, and I
groaned.

In the night, my husband
speaks of surrender

to the things we are waiting for
that are very close.

*

A body, I remember his body.
(Going to be with my
husband, again.)

Writing about Job,
and reading a "great book"
he said

"I have never understood
religion before."

*

Rembrandt's *Three Trees*.

They are, some say, meant to be
the three crosses, but

they could be any
three trees.

(The meaning I attach to.)

I pretended I was a scholar.

Why do I always think
I have to read more,
study more.

*

Never brave enough to say—
this is what I am doing now.

I could give my attention.
I could offer in exchange.

*

I do not fault
those holy figures
seeking
a method

and I forgive
my own misguided attempts.

This morning,
her living body laid out before me,

I asked,
Is this the place of happiness?

*

Three windows of light.

Always the beam of light,
wherever it may fall in the room…

She studies the streak of light.

A Burning

What I thought would make me happy:
the image of that
falls away now—
the *image.*

In the night
I began to see.
I realized I was not
worried about
anything.

Her head between my hands.
I am a presence.

Help me stand still.
Then the power.
Then the sky.

All the things I could say—
that come to me
(but keep pushing):
say more. Look at it more. And then,
stop looking.

Evening Song

In the evening
the world opens up.

The plane of the vast sky, all the waters.
On the fiery earth,
all human emotion.

And who would climb out?

All new creatures born,
born in this day—
the evening surveys

how the day has been
(and what has really been seen).

A small voice, crying its own way...

Perhaps tonight, only the crickets;
the barking of a dog;
focused intensely by the texture of air...

Who has not known the calling—
and closed her eyes to listen?

Sleep, little one.

Seemingly alone, but the nearness.

Deep, Abiding

I was waiting for when
the acceptance would come.

These are the things I have seen about myself.
Her body took form.

And for this I had to wait.

For Little Bodies Bodily Thrones: For Spirits Invisible

She's in need of more
comfort than I.

I could hear the birds, still
as in my other life—
and I remember that there had been
a life even before that
and not always
a happy one.

So I had to learn contentment—for
how could I give
what I did not have?

In the labor was a kind of
deep meditation.
The one breath, the one push,
as far as I could go…

when the doctors said:
essential—to get her
out of there—

now: this universe—
opening to me.

Viva Vox

Every time I looked out the window,
there was a different kind of light.

I remember other things, of course
but it is the only thing
I felt in that blinding way.

In the pain, I said,
What is the happiness?

I've never been so pure,
I said…

felt it to open up—
the agony—
like the flower
precarious on the counter.

How She Moves Her Hand

If I could see a still life,
I would see it changing.

She is more fluid than I
and calls to me.
(We are different objects now.)

It is the only thing
happening—this moment:
so small the circle of her curving.

With a terror
I let those
bits and pieces go
(the trivial)

to flow into the image
to burn

into another world
where I am not known.

In the night, where I am,
I don't need to be a figure.

Everything Was Moving, And Not

The figure was not my mother,
but a woman
in a long lavender gown.

She placed
a rectangular painting of trees
on my breast—
hung on a
beaded silver chain.

I had thought it meant
one thing—
and when the disappointment came
I knew
it must now mean another.

She came out looking
differently
than expected—
which made me curious, watchful.

As Though I Were Awakening From A Sleep

Last night I went to sleep
by the sallow candle.

Dream of the other children.

The first, alabaster white,
I carried in my arms
through a door.

The other two were restless.
They rose up for an instant,
and then
they were sleeping in their beds

in front of my house by the tree.

And the fields opened up
to show my mother,
not in illness, or death,
shining white.

Anamnesis

One is worried that they are going to be
cut away.
And then one is worried that one will be cut.

*

In the brown chair,
speaking to me:
a soul
I had been waiting for.

(It would be out of time.)

And it is myself speaking to it.
And this is not a dream

when I couldn't touch him.

*

He said—after his great fatigue—
after many months

he acquired fluidity

that came with more ease
than he had ever known
and of its own
accord.

*

I could hardly speak

when the doctors would examine their bodies
when they would cut.

It was only by love

the argument being not
that love evaporates
but that it is *there*
as I am.

*

Had I been trying to make something
other than it was?

It was a particular hunger.

How could I stop the suffering?
And what would come to replace it?

My Fortieth Year

Walking through the world—
like a curator—beauty and form—
brokenness, the earth.

You will never see the sky
like that again.

At the end of something—
innocent of myself.

A particular light, a white light,
a definite light, not glory.

Offering The Agony

What is the world here?
What am I thinking of?
As if the world
had been flipped
in my mind—which was
the vision. No longer
obsession,
my feeling emerged
a different passion—
not anything I had known.
Leaving the exile,
my body exhausted
screamed for rest
and the mind, unable to think
in that unravelling and ravelling of thought
could merely look—
barely to take the picture in.

Mysterium Tremendum

1.

I am weak—
but why isn't that a joy?

And why have I forgotten to say,

I have worked hard,
it was my gift.

(With every weakness
comes a thought.)

Perhaps only exhaustion
could take me there.
This is my body.

I study my hands, and what to do with them.
His words, in bed, a comfort.

2.

The color of the earth
seems meaningful today.
Where else had I seen that—
what other place?

The day in the lavender garden.
Many days, in childhood.

The girls doing Latin lessons
please me when I go for a walk,

having come to light
all those images of tender children.

What had bothered me
seemed a distant thing.

The river was *alive* and *frolicking*.

I would like to be a beautiful
old woman.

3.

The roses were cut so
severely
in nakedness.
Few leaves on the trees
but the earth is promising. I look outside
at the desolate garden.

The baby sleeps in my arms.
Everything is moving gently now,
and I am still.

Why did it happen that way?

What beauty alive in her face?

4.

Her voice in the night. Her voice
in the morning.

Her gift to me is greater.
Standing on the edge of it.
(I did not know
that I knew
such depth of
feeling.)

Losing him was only my fear,

but in my weepiness, tenderness,
I couldn't bear
to speak of losing him.
(The X-ray of pain.)

He speaks of his death—
and what a widow said.

I had only known death
as devastating. (Half
an emotion.)

And he said, as her husband had,
he wanted me to live my life,
love someone.

She looked like a woman in a
beautiful painting. Pale,
wrapped in the dark.

I keep coming home
expecting what?

We go out
into the fresh air
and the air (always) changes—

and then there's the three of us.

What He Brings Me In The Morning

Michael is standing here
(with coffee and croissants).

Now the light in which I see him
has come to me
out of dark morning

and I see him as a child again

preparing to greet her.

Under The Tall Trees

Staring at the light green trees—

(perhaps this is what they mean)
going into the garden, refuge—

little bird being alive.

The sun is not so blinding here.
Shadow on a pillar,
on a high wall.

I am thinking of
the sensation of skin—
the learning of touch, of texture.
I do feel more peaceful.
(My fitfulness finally ripped out.)

Will there always be a center?

I was looking up and the sky was (going) red.

Human Documents

What in this world?
I was watching a painter

and his method of painting.
He used black and white, and a kind of grey—
and out of it rose a form of color:
the earth.

He lived by the river.
Studied its light.

*

Always a self,
however fleeting

today as I watched the pepper trees,
I thought the realm of the spirit, the realm of matter

is not *reveal yourself.*
They are myself—herself...

Stand back in awe—
and let it become itself.

The ideal can hinder a thing.

*

These things make their impressions.
The moment is not lost

when she startled, became so still—
as if to recognize a voice,
as if she recognized our soothing song.
What the time then means now.

That was another kind of work
(I had never done before):

We were singing to calm ourselves.
We were steadying our hands.

*

When I met him I had a dream

not calling me back, not forward,
but here, strange presence.

House stirring,
and I am up.

*

Oh the pettiness
happening
out of order

in the dream of the closed, partially opened door
(light can contain terror)

behind which we are beyond ourselves in the dark

and the three of us
do nothing more than

float in the water
and look at the stars.

In A Museum

Portrait of a merchant, of his wife, of
Jesus raising Lazarus from the dead…

She likes Russian peasant—
of all the ones she can select—
and clutches her postcard.

A red nose, a particular red ugliness.

She wants to hop on all the benches—to lie down
and look at the ceiling.

She wants to wander, to roam.

*

Sitting in the corner
with the European photographs—

for many years I lived there.

And how different I am, in this,
than I was.
How different the picture,
the color, the light.

The red walls.
To be in a room with museum red walls…

Though I had always felt
this restlessness come upon me…

And then the calm.

*

Yellow light on a rose bush—
what caught my eye
made me look at it.

The ways she moves
could be lost.

The way he speaks to me.

Where did my capacity come from?

Singing as a child?
Singing for no
particular reason?

With them
just to dwell.

The View Of The World As She Sees It

A flower, at the market,
wrapped in brown paper.

She hugs it because it is her flower.

The leaves tinged with brown,
the flower, already starting to wilt—
but glorious in her eyes.

It seems clear, pure—
(not as in one thing, not as in my idea of child)
but as in
utterly human

which, too, gives rise
to the beauty—
yellow and strange:

offering it back to me.

The Air When She Turns Three

What I see is the excitement of

the animals become
just a little wild
as they frolic about
waiting for their dinner:

their delight and their restlessness
at seeing the keeper.

And the tender care toward the sick pig
sequestered in her refuge:

the sick pig that
the other day blew an enormous pig booger
on my daughter's sleeve
(and thus acquired fame).

The keeper lets
my daughter's little hands
plunge a waffle cone into the pen

as he speaks so graciously to her,

as if each question and explanation were
the first thing cast
upon the air.

And the light comes—

the light when they close the pumpkin patch
and the vegetable guy is pulling away in his
blue truck.
It is late, and I lift her up

to look out
at the mountains.

We are looking at each other
in the purple light

like my first and earlier vision
to gaze upon her face.

Celestial Room

I remember when I was four
a book seemed from heaven
and then, when I was eight,
it seemed a field.

*

How large the world has become;
the thoughts, capable.
I wanted to look at that, just that.

*

I thought I would never speak again.

But there are books, transformed,
and souls
taking time to recognize
the speaking, and which voice.

Works And Days

I read a word. Look up
a word.

I would like to get nearer
for intimacy, for touch.

The leaves moving down the street.
The leaves still.

Change me as you will.
Change the words.

Restive

Why did the soul come now?
                    It came for contemplation.
The spirits of the living,
of what interests me.

Show me what you would have me do.
                    Be idle.

Mirae Speculationes

1.

The print of "The Fly"
in terra cotta
hovers in the kitchen

if I live or if I die

the two panels
pressed together in the frame

and I have always felt the need
to separate them
and change the border to a blazing white.

2.

You're not mute
You shouldn't be mute

I felt it was time.
(I could not see you the same.)

I have come to look at your face.

Leaving The Rest Unseen

Out for his walk, now.
I am in my study.
It is evening—and she sleeps.

If it were only this day
I see and feel, it is enough.

Break it open, my heart.

*

This is the refuge now—on the ground,
the place where I am growing these feelings

I fell to the ground.
And you were returned to me.

What is it that carries love?
Where I learned love

the ache for body
will only answer to
what was, for me,

the particular.

An Ancient Face

I stayed up late at night
because I wanted to wonder.

What is the fear?
That I'm somehow not living?
But haven't you taught me this life?

In secret, between us, oh, joy!
What seemed not
was a very deep place.

Red chair.
The long sky.
(What I have always known.)
And all the beautiful creatures surround.

Creature Feeling

And perhaps the element that the child
can't possess yet—what the child is not capable of yet—

her little orange crown
instructs me
in style, then touch

what she likes, what she doesn't like.
(What I wouldn't deny her.)

What would I say?
That I was happy

when she raises the brush above
and plunges mercilessly into the vat of color
(nothing to hold back).

Museum We Enter Again

The good dragon, the phoenix bird
(story on a tile, on a scroll):

the words hadn't been part of their history and
they wanted to have them
written in.

*

There were days I had destroyed
thinking them
unfit, undone—but the cry is always the same.

As we enter the sculpture piece,
the stones, she asks,
"How did it get up there
without falling?"

Touching the face
of the pale figure,
wandering in the yard of
chisels and saws.

Night Watch

...the gaze attempting to recover blindness by a dazzling flash, precisely at its outer limit and even just a bit before, where it would surprise itself at the instant of seeing, where it would see itself see.

—Louis Marin

1.

What is the voice that is speaking?
(It wasn't a book.)

I felt I went on a journey—
not toward you

but myself—
and this is how I came nearer to you.

2.

Who is walking through the room?
It is a room.

Somebody else's room—and I was going
to walk through it.

I was leveled to
the beauty of it—
like another place of life—
that had been hidden from me.

It was a relief

there are no figures here.
And no sun.

3.

Leaving one room and
entering another,

a room in which I was familiar with
(somehow—
of crossing, of exchange)

the windows, the walls,
the bed:

all that light would rise up
how a soul passes through.

What is it that I am?
What is it before you?

4.

Did you think I didn't know the dark?

When he said, "It's your way
of being in the world..."

I don't even know where the voice came from.
A thing so lovely—
this was presence.

I don't care what the masters say.

5.

And when I told the story
I was myself—

the changing of
perception
of soul—taking me somewhere.

I will not be ashamed of it—
how much I loved them.

A song, a memory, I would sing it.

6.

What I was saying about love

as if the two worlds
were coming together—

but what in this world
was I raising up?

The calling—the utter raw
longing

I was always going to come back to
and I should say it in the room:

I will be alive,
and I will face you.

And I will look at the room
being in the room,
filling it.

The Day With Both Of Them

By the window
in the fancy hotel—
looking out, looking out with them.

A little coffee. A little cake.

These things have come for me.

And not a secret, but apparent
from which I come out of

how I could
stand back, and let happen

the birds, and the sea,
and the sky.

I woke up this morning
and I saw the light—

and I thought—I like living here
in the crystal grey

and I understood I would never
be the same.

What passes through me
gains a residence

as if I were some small vibrating figure:
the creatures seem vivid to me,
burnished in flame.

Correspondence With The Heavens

It is such a simple thing—
now—since I am so in need of it myself

of which I lacked for myself—
so I gave it—and it came to me

what was given to me:
this love.

Planting wildflowers with my daughter,
I have no idea what I am doing.

But they are wild, aren't they?
They do intend to grow?

Uncreated Light

In memory of my family

David Gildroy (1959–1984)
Donald Gildroy (1930–1990)
Douglas Gildroy (1969–2005)
Donna Gildroy (1932–2007)

In The Chamber Of The Voices

Douglas Gildroy
(August 18, 1969—January 23, 2005)

1.

I don't know how to speak to you
since you are in your other self

but I am speaking since
so much life is lived that way.
I will speak to the ground.

You are so expert in death.
With so much to show me.

I have learned not to presume with you

when you wanted to speak
to me. It is true
I was called back to part of you
which you know is that part of me
in our blood.

All summer long, I was with you.

2.

You let them in—by your departure
and now there was a chasm—
and I had to go in
between the echoing walls.

Who are these strangers?
Everyone is speaking about you.

What they could talk about—
what happens in this life—
always more details.

To those lost to us

I'll cast my voice

as did our father
so many years ago

at our older brother's gravestone
saying, *God Bless you, son.*

3.

I don't know about the eternal order of things—

I have always bumbled
there—the ideas
shrouded me—

but I've tried
to remember to speak

what comes to me.
What comes for me like no other

was the thing in the end
I trusted.

I could be sure of what came out of my mouth.

I can speak to you
only from this side
but don't voices travel?

If I could make the words real,
make them cut,

I would get through to
the chamber of the voices.

4.

When I entered the book of the dead
you brought me here.

Others have brought me to the edge.
I have come looking.

This is our story

of the always surprise of

how this was not the story
we would have wanted

and look
there are other places
in us—separated.

But here we cross over—
hand in hand.

Give me your glimpse.
I give you my release.

5.

When it occurs to me
that this is grief—

a vision of two severed—

the world changed.
Now I see there are two worlds.

They are (so) beautiful—

the figures that move.

The mind can turn
when it sees the soul
in its world.

Release unto death, the book said.
And you came to me
after hearing my words.

And it shivered out of my body—
that grief—carried so long—

we were living—where we were.
I could feel you—
and not the grief.

6.

I don't know where they buried you.
You've been taken.

Yet I think you are the only one
who understands my grief.

In the earth—
who will lie next to our father?

But how could you not hear me—
how could that spirit not turn—
to one who holds your image:
a child at play.

Once I heard
a voice in my head
that said
write these words,
I would lay me down in the field.

And I heard our
father's voice say,
Don't go.

7.

The door to my house is red, now.
Today I'm painting the house.

For years, confusion and shame.

Oh, I am not in the realm of judgment.

Come with me, my brother, my little one.
Come to this grief

as all young children wail.

What to say over your body?

We will sit on this little ladder, blazing.

The Funeral In My Head

I see what I have to do.
It's in the chasm.
I must rest there
a while.

I have had a hard time waiting,
so I will wait some more.

There is the image that is not the truth,
the one to not hold,
the one to not let cling
in all its utter blinding:

what I would say,
the people we would be.

I'm afraid this means I need it

to turn back solemnly
toward day.

The Field

Little field, where our older brother built a fort.
Wild kept, and the railroad tracks. We'd run over the tracks so fearful
past Shasta and Beechnut Gum to climb
the train watch tower.
What is occurring there, that childhood place?
So far from here
where they found your body.
And this field—where the sweet children run—
hiking down to cliffs
sliding down—
to the place where they can hold
the caterpillars green and gold:
my daughter runs to tell me
she has held one as in
my stories to her of when I was a little girl—
I held one in my outstretched hands.
What is down there?
As I sit in the circle of tree stumps
looking out.
Could be occurring anywhere,
but I am here.
My field—
I always thought of it as our field.
I know you felt I left you
in that house. Long ago—
before the tall golden grasses were cut.

In The Book Of Love, For The Not Living

I could even imagine
a kind of angel.
For years
he remained hazy.

One suicide
flanking my side. One brother.

Break it once, break it twice

and my other
brother
flies around
to my other side—
enveloping me,
enclosing.

But there are no wings.

And I have to finally
turn and say

I don't know the agonies of your life.

In The Heat, The Body

The temperature cranked in the house,
last heat for your body.

The bones in your wrists began
to speak as bones.

A soul turned to tell:
this is what the body has done.

So cold, so cold.

I will look to it, to this that is real,
to send you to your future.

It was by the smell of you
the neighbors found you.

One naked mattress on the floor.

Blue Partridge

Childhood home.
Little bird
I'll never see again.
My mind said, Never go in.

It was my older brother's blue partridge, mine was red,
hung on the Christmas tree, stored in the cedar closet my father
built in the basement, under the
stairs. Where is it now?
In my memory,
where does it go?

In the aftermath,
what has been left to me:

the stages of dark,
the stages of light,
what happened in what world.

And what could I say beyond
our father's message when we were children:
go live,
go into the world—
do not fear its beauty.

Maybe they have compassion on me, too—
when my two dead brothers meet. Still so young.

When I can't breathe
in the house with broken windows.

Uncreated Light

Yours was the death, yours was the dying.

I found you in
the pauper's field

and something sang through me
(if there
ever was a song)—
which I could
speak to myself, very quietly,
and move along.

Oh in my heart,
do you not think I am a part of this?

Bless the failure, bless the flame,
bless my fruitless attempt,
the shame.

And what do I do with this love,
that sticks like pitch to my heart—and will never
let me go.

Why I am standing in your image.
Do not try to change it—
to turn it into something
joyous and free—
you are here—you are gone—
dead—
uncreated light.

A Chorus

1. *Dementia*

As if she were my mother and not my mother,
as if we have stepped into the other world—and are now speaking

at the hospital, at the home,
at the room
in which nothing goes on.

And she hovers. Half here,
half in her other mind.

Perhaps half in memory—
my mother is
painting in the basement
in stark light,
happily.

I think they were daisies.

Those are the flowers for me.

The painting
what she was looking for

as just the person she happened to be.

2.

When I realized I couldn't go near

it was not that I did not

want to call to you—there—like some
higher mother—

but we
could not meet that way—
face to face—

so I sent a voice out
and I sat dearly listening.

3.

I did not grasp how I have missed you—
as if only now I see
I could let myself feel

what has been missed.

Where will you be going now?

The grief we must go into,
mother and child.

I have this voice you've given me.
You must know this.

The children wrapping ribbons around
the maypole.
My child
whom you've never seen.
The spring.

In My Mind, The Idea Of House

Traveling above,
as the earth shifts:
a plate of the earth.

I was afraid of what I saw

that made the soul
that made me.

*

Ah, the room smells good—
my room when I was a little girl—
opening the shutters my father made,
the little desk.

White handkerchiefs on the
ironing board,
my doll.

Clean,
how I loved the days of cleaning,
of painting the rooms in summer.

Oh, evocation of my father,
your husband washing the walls.

*

I was down in the basement.
The quiet with nothing in it. What I didn't
know was there clinging
like a family memory in the snow.

For me—do you think that's sweet? It's a
brutal image. I can't tell you how
much life it took out of me to live.

*

Looking down
over the bodies.
It seems to me
physical directions

will take me down into the earth.

I have to face the real
to climb out of it—
to see the other real—
which is also a truth.

Let us all speak freely, Oh my brothers,
to be done with shame.
What is love, what is brutal acceptance?

*

I speak to the dead, the demented.

Father, mother.

Maybe today
I will write down—
appliances ripped out.

How you my mother kept going back in—
past the porch rails—broken off—

no tables—no chairs—
graffiti covering the walls.

Until a truck came to take you to safety—
until the yellow tape
cautioned off—
a drug house:
Hazardous Waste.

Then nothing. Nothing.

No paintings. And no photographs of my
father to be found.

I dreamt a carnival game.
The red chips disappearing
as our home was being played and played away.

In The Open Field

In the melting emptiness,
the heart of ice.

And then there were the birds,

and then the light.
An upward movement.

The bringing in,
in the field in which
I did follow,
where the souls meet.

In the circle,
these were the people
who were my family,
the four of them.

They were swaying,
and I was scared.
How I would sing a little song—
the voice of the little song—
to keep going back in.

Then I saw
in the middle of the grief
there was the heart of grief,
raw love.

It Is Night, In My Study

The day of feeling awful,
of what has come out of me

and flying out of me—
in mistake—in grief—

but I have always yearned

for that other.
I have always felt that pull.

*

A recording of the times I sit.

How I carried my father's voice:
"Don't forget where you came from."

Those voices?
What I came from?

I don't know what to do with this
part of myself,

this work
to tunnel me through to what

I trust.

*

I am staying here—
to not be looking away.

When I finish waiting in quiet
I feel that this is where I am to be.

*

What I couldn't say and be—
I will say now.

I wanted my voice to go somewhere.

Here I give it to you—
whoever you are—
into your hands—
into your mind.

And when my death comes—
what will I be filled with?

I don't want to write about the dead, I said.

Then write about the living.

The Child's Dreams

Her drawing of the angel of fire,
the candle's red flame, her delicate crown.

"The child's dreams," my daughter says.

How I am listening.

Go back into that mind—
that's where I have to meet them.

If they are children of God
and death does not take them to God?

And at the divide—
a landscape (where my daughter takes me).

How the figures frolic,
how they play—how they manage to
delight the day.
Oh light—oh light—
come in.

I Will Perform The Exercise

And I entered the room.

A candle was burning.

The teacher placed my hands
up to
my daughter's
hands
as she said the words—

the words the teacher had taught her—

showing me the movements,
singing me the songs.

*

I will perform the exercise

as a way to begin,

and say
a blessing
into the blessed order of things.

My daughter watches
as I move with the teacher

to flow, to extend.
This the dance we're supposed to learn:
I don't control you—
and you don't control me,
she says.

*

I will go there myself

to the source of light—
whatever that may be.

To help my daughter's movement in this world—
her sense of balance,
her body's grace.

We will practice
before bedtime.

Slumber my little one, slumber my pretty one...
moves through the air

and it's not dark.

*

And I finally know
what to say.

I am speaking it—
I am saying it over our bodies.

As I reach my body up,
in the night—
she follows.

There is beauty before us.
There is beauty behind us...

It is time for me to love strongly.

The Fennel In The Garden Grows High

Maybe the walk isn't sweet and lovely.

Maybe here a brick,
there a brick,
rubbish, broken.

What I was meeting
in the open air—

I who thought only
childhood and suffering

in the open air—

I am not there
any longer.

Brother, brother
come to me—

gather, gather
round the tree—

in the grove we walk

inviting
no wound,

no sound.

Ah, my restless one, Ah, my anguished soul—
lie down, lie down

in the tall golden grasses
reaching up.

Let us gather the children,
my mother says sweetly.

We will become

something different
together.

Temple Hymn

If I delight, I will not harm.
And forget my self
into being.

I have been looking all over for the beauty.

Pray for the beauty. Pray for the light.
Any small thing.

The yellow mustard seed
refracts
the field

swaying

this voice
that has fallen to me.

If I Kiss Your Forehead

Donna Gildroy
(August 16, 1933—February 17, 2007)

My daughter brings me her drawing
of a tree. To console me.

In the grief which almost breaks me
as I kneel by your casket.

She is relieved I am not crying—
my crying is strange for her—

but I cannot hide
what convulses the body:

it is not her grief
as I rise
except that it is mine

except that you are
my
mother—

this much she understands

although you never wanted to know her.

If I kiss your forehead
it is not to say goodbye.

Why I feel you still alive.

Not lost to me in all this time.

What happened in our life.
This blank grief.

Family Photographs

1.

When I see the family photographs—

rejoining me to that other life

that then stops.

What is it like to be the only one left?
No one says it.

Should I remember every dress I wore?

as I look at my young woman self
looking out

there with my cousin Peggy
with all my other cousins

in the photo
my aunt gives me.

2.

And my exhaustion at death.

It was so hard
to stand clear
with all the calla lilies

that reappear in
my parents' wedding photo—

the only one I have

that Joe, my father's best friend
kindly brings to me.

He is telling me his story.

The story in which everyone
has some part

to tell

one after another

of the secrets
of her life
which we are surprised
to hear,
and then, not.

How she would only call anyone
when everyone was out of the house.

How she could have had another life.

Joe shows me pictures of him
and Dale and my mother—
the old friends
out to dinner,
smiling.

3.

Bill Fitzgerald—who went to first grade
with my mother—

greets me from McKinley Park—
from the
"old neighborhood."

My aunt says his family had a reputation
for kind deeds.

As Erinn,
my childhood friend

comes to tell me of the
"video of the bike"
she found:

me teaching
my little brother to ride.

I was running down the street
beside him, and he
was riding

all openness, in the
air.

4.

The family fell apart, Joe tells my husband,
after my father died.

My father sits
in the big green chair.

He keeps asking—
with the same distant stare—

what did I do wrong?
How has this come into my house?

5.

My daughter knows it's solemn
in the "death room" she says,

when my husband has to
quiet her,

but she is busy
on a unicorn walk

as she pulls her stuffed unicorn
behind her and beckons
my aunts Rose and Maureen
to follow

her in her long golden dress:
in her long golden dress
she flows and
sings her
made-up song.

Though I Walk Through The Valley

When the priest asks me to speak
about what gave you joy:

in my time to speak
before you publicly

in the time to recite
the twenty-third psalm

which I remember you loved
and hung on David's bedroom wall.

Your body,
the being there,
the speaking.

The beautiful photos behind me—

I wanted to take the time
to recall our dead,

I wanted to take the time to say it:

my father, Donald;
my brother, David; my brother, Douglas.

And you, Donna.

What is the memory?

the word
the word we do say

the voice that does not go away

the one at the heart of the heart.

Clear Instrument

It is not that the body looks peaceful
in any given way—
but that the face is
beautiful.

I haven't seen you in so long.

This is as far as I have advanced—
and without the striving, now—
I would look at you
in this small time
left to me—

if that is surrender—
if this is

what I have to say to you.

I will accept your love as I am—

since it is a part of me.

Green Lion

Not anything hidden from my daughter
as we wander the city—to
distraction.

My daughter loves the large wet messy
snowflakes in the tree
in the park outside the hotel,
within the iron rails.

It is snowing again
in Chicago.
Here where my father
took my photograph
so long ago
at the door of the museum

and, as she leaps to touch the green lion,
she pulls and pats its tail

at the door of the museum.

As we wandered

I decided to follow

the long
red paper dragon

I had waited for her
to make,

to see her run
from
window to window

in the hall of the miniatures: tiny
bedrooms, tiny
kitchens

she stood and stared at,
the architecture
of the tiny
church

gilded in gold,

and the long
red paper dragon
trailing behind her

back to our
home in California, to
the future.

To turn my face—
I felt myself floating—

and the green lion, which I have loved,
which I will always love,

transmuted in memory now
because she touched it.

In The Light (The Haze) Of The Field

If I sit here long enough

maybe I will hear

if the field is dry
all they wouldn't tell me.

If the field is clear.

My grief is great

when I try to find out

which is the essential

in the what I will never know.

Not clouded because
I am in it

but from a long distance off
and then in

a little girl,
a little body

in the daring glance back
longing for the dead.

A Requiem For The Self

Is what I am defined?

If I could go to that other place
and meet.

If I could say something
over the body

to help it.

What would she like me to say?

When I fell asleep

I believed we could perceive
each other

in something beyond me—
terrifying light—

lifting the pressure out of me—
up into the air above the bed

as if my whole soul opened
and I was walking

in spite of myself,
in spite of my self that would sleep.

Every Time I Am Gentle

It is a kind of forgiveness of myself
for not being able to save for them
another fate.

This morning the mourning dove woke me—and
I thought it was my daughter calling
mommy, mommy.

The light like
the light blue jacket—

"powder blue" she said,

"velour"
was her request—

that I sent my mother
because she was cold.

A Picture Of The Universe

I am so tired of that other world—
why must it intrude?

The struggles of the day—
what are they?

Everything moves around.

My daughter says—
I'll see if I like my God.

Redrawing God's nose,

she draws the world, the universe,
the dark, the rainbow, God and the angels,

the lake in Chicago a vivid blue.

*

I know I was not meant
to be in that world—

but this doesn't mean
I don't miss it.

What it means
in the life of the soul—

not the sorting of good
and evil and all the
implications—

but what I say and send
in all full reality

if the universe be
merciful

is my life
that will come from here.

*

Some call this feeling
good.

At my desk
and my husband comes in
to kiss me good morning.

Behind me my daughter unfolds
her accordion-like journal
that opens and opens and opens
one long piece of
rice paper
fold after delicate fold:

God and his three angels
where everything flows

even in the black and grey.

*

And as I live my life

how little I have understood
our grief—
how little I have understood
so much more—this joy.

The book of the dead says
one should be happy—

it will send them on their way.

And I Would Hold You In My Arms

I laid open my grief,
my utter confusion,
my weakness, my shame,

and the intuition
slipped in so
unexpectedly—

I was holding my husband in my arms.

For so long—
emotion long carried—and hid—

and now it comes out of me—

I was trying so hard to live,

I couldn't help myself—
as if the will to live
spoke through us all.

Night Bird

What felt real in my hands—working—
kin to the self

when I was sitting here
unassuming

the unknown things:

what is a voice
what did I follow
what did I see there.

The night bird sings
to touch that world.

Thing of beauty—
to be able to take it in.

It would not be loving

if we did not
become ourselves

and something else I haven't dreamed of yet.

Architecture Of Light

And what to do with them
when they reappear
in my mind?

When the human
confusion
has been cleared away

in the light that persists—
what is it we are looking at?

In the cafe
there's a box of light
overhead,
window of sky

where a square of blue
and the middle parts of trees
show through,

and next to me the
vines grow
and the light hits the white bark

refracting off
shadows of leaves on the ground—

a strange and pure light
that sometimes touches

the children eating breakfast,
people and dogs,

the business of the day

in which we are all walking around.

This morning,
I ached for the sky—
the light I like to see—
but not too direct

and here I am covered
in the structure
where the outside is let in

breezy and clean,
that lets me see it more

while I feel
it beaming down on me.

With Friends In Provincetown

—for Michael Mazur (1935—2009)

Because our daughter exclaims
she wants to be an artist

after hours of drawing
with pastels
at dinner

he replies, *If I am still around*
I will help you.

Then turns, and says,
but you won't need me.

In his studio
where we have been taken in
on this side of the landscape—this Atlantic ocean—

after running around
all day long
watching John and Harry running at the beach
with the dogs

and breakfast with Mar Mar and Cleopatra
at our favorite café,

our daughter chases Gail's cats
in and out

as we all stand with the doors wide open.

And tonight on the flats

the light we see
seems the only
real light.

The palette covered
with years of paint—

the color, the materials—

as he opens
cabinet drawers

and pulls out
paintings

until

blue with
yellow at its center

that lights it up
all luminosity

my daughter says
"that is so beautiful"

and in one sweeping gesture
his face beaming down on her

he gives it to her

in childlike
delight.

Looking Into The Natural Order

Because I have come to understand
they will open the world for me—

I have opened the world.

*

I dream of seeing my mother

painting
the light on the flats.

I am afraid of the ocean (but I am here)—
and what it is going to tell me.

Potential of light, of
beauty.

*

Looking into the natural order—
looking at what the creatures do,

what is blocked to us

by us.

I feel the same way I
feel at a funeral.

The experience
of grief,

changed
in me,

shame, then rest
in the yard.

*

My daughter draws in her bird journal,
walking out on the rocks,
by our guest apartment by the sea.

We are looking at all the new birds we can see,
delighted by the creatures
different stirrings.

Wouldn't it be nice if the bird was
soaring

where my soul sees

whatever comes to me?

Cello Lessons

What they are working at—
her strength, and her bow-—

the deep note,
the chord.

In this room.

As my daughter jokes with the teacher
letting her be that way, sending her on her way.

How is it that I am mother
to this child?

In the dream of the death cell:
the medicine I had to take

emerges in me
yellow, orange, and light.

Maybe it's all the souls that I feel.

Maybe it
is
light.

Could I Have Opened My Eyes Without You

—for my husband

It's a little joke, you make,
about my next husband,

if you are ever gone—

because you think
I should be loved.

But don't you know me?

I know—know what I've been given.

I've been trained
for grief

but this life
has blinded me into the living world—

of the permeated.

And what she is. Our child. Not perfect.
Not anything else but herself.
Unimpeded—allowed to be.

And this is why I get to look.
All my humanness turned to gift.

When My Daughter Speaks Of The Heavenly Meadows

The little black and white bird
she saw dying and then dead
in the bluffs
and said two blessings for

will go to her—
and the butterfly that she held to not
get stuck in the wires.

My daughter attends to a rose.
For her, it's a rose.
For me, it's something surviving

in the garden.

If I am to open my heart—
to the grain, and stick, and flower.

She says she was playing with the children
in the heavenly meadows
until it was her time
to come down.
Until she saw me, she says.

Labyrinth On My Table

And the light from the opening of this book has made me find what is mine and remain in this.

—Marguerite Porete (?—1310), *The Mirror of Simple Souls*

Marguerite Speaks

I don’t need it to be the voice of God.

It’s the voice. I know it.

Let’s not argue about it like a
virtue.

The Voice

I am completely flung on you—

this chasm

between us in the asking—

what I know:
the abyss of God.

(With love,
the rest does not matter.)

Help me stop
and wait

then speak as it does.

The Being Toward Which She Tends

You opened a door—
I didn't know
could open—
didn't know existed—
now forever changed—

because you are no longer idea—
a distant vision—

but something that
attached
to my solar plexus

and each step I take
forward—
this is not
thinking about my life—

this is in it—
thrust to the earth
I have landed—
however my life moves

and your hand is always touching it.

Aperture

The window opened,
the door,
the sky was open to me, clear
and the leaves of the trees
kept nodding that everything was all right—
I was moving along
and all was with me.

A Desperate Attempt At Beauty

1.

You know I am not strong enough.

The dark is always with us, I know.

Though I don't even know
what you are—

this pace we keep
into the unknown

except for intimacy of how you touch
membrane most real

and beauty attaches.

I breathe.

The difficulty in
just breathing.

How can I get to you?

(Everybody I know

if asked

has trouble breathing.)

2.

What is it like
to walk upon the earth?

No longer living muted and alone,

opening the book that is my life.

Its voice awoke in me

and I landed in the present

to go out looking at the world.

You are making beauty
in the world:

audacious task.

3.

In the archeological digs
looking, looking—

if I could find out where I am in this—

the architectural locations

of a fully realized
internal landscape

embody my mind-

locator of beauty.

When I feel full,

the facts do not match the

soul.

Vast
the angel.

4.

This thing in the air—
vapor on the paper.

Flat out I will
say:

it's a conversation.

Oh! my voice!

My heart is excoriated.

My mind says I have a love affair
with this voice—

the voice
that can no longer be contained.

5.

Today I thought:
I am done with suffering.

When the elders came to speak to me

I told them

to inquire into beauty—
and let our inquiry be a response to beauty.

Trees—to make a picture
in the mind
the grove of trees—

but the image was there
already

like a grove I had once walked by

out of the corner of my eye

which seeps through.

6.

This is not to say nothing happened.

What happened, I do not know.

My voice, this way

or be false
which kills everything—

the sweet peas in the garden,

that light (on any face).

The true voice—
I heard it.

Relieve me of the burden

(that I am)

saying it wrong.

7.

I will try
to appear

though I feel nauseated.

Oh, not that way

to be so close
excruciating
obliterating
exquisite

into other being.

I want to make my gift.

I am crushed

when all I wanted

was to stand by
the tree

and speak

walking, feeling, light.

8.

Even here I am
disappointed in myself

when the voice of me squats and says
love me, love me, love me

I would open myself

pure, chiseled, exquisite

to see the true voice.

Of The Work Of Love And Why She Has This Book Made

For five minutes I sat down under a tree
and made myself

think about

how much I am loved—

which felt ridiculous—
wasteful of worldly time

fraught with the ludicrous gesture,

that being loved would indeed
change anything—

then the voice reached in
and grabbed

my heart open

and I excavated love
from a raw thought.

Her Professed Religion

How could you not know
how close you were?

Stepping up
to who I am.

I don't want to doubt myself,
but to emerge.

All this is so that
I would say it.

Am I speaking?

The physical, mystical body

the place I am working in.

Let us speak of this matter of tarrying.

Today I thought
I know where my body is.

I feel my feet on the ground.

More Free, And Very Free

I am here, and here is the life
I am given to do.

You are going to have to live your way,

and speak yourself

what comes from the inner landscape of beauty.

Not about approval,
this world.

So if I contain thought in matter,

but speaking is another matter.

Nothing Other Than To See

The inner landscape of beauty,
how does it get here?

I see the beginning of the vision—

what we engage with
takes us.

What is the length of visible light?

I don't know what I wanted?

No.

I wanted to see beauty and more of it.

Like Wax From A Seal

I have been looking for you

the place where the soul says

this is home
my particular home
and nobody else's

the place where I fit
made for feeling, for sense

from which all knowing has emanated

the honing system
like a radar leading me
through my life

that tells me

I would like to speak like this

and this is who I love.

Labyrinth On My Table

Here I walk around
thinking no one will listen.

I don't know how to without you

chiseling the self.

A structure I built around myself—
inside, outside
like an interior castle.

I remember walking by the castle.

All those trees and leaves

quietly
patiently listening

until I was able.

(Things in the world—
when I was not in pain.)

The quieted voice, now happy.

Ravishing Farnearness

Oh, please be near!
It's the feeling I am trying
and not getting here somehow—
my own shakiness,
unearthed?
As if my earth shook and I was
unstable—no—up?

To know you know
to know I am not anything
other than I am
not you—
nor distinction

of the feeling that something
is seriously wrong—

when this place in me is
opened up.
Unearthing.

So where am I
standing?
(I rather liked the ground.)

The fragility of the yet
unformed

that is in me—
of me—
is me—who's pretending anymore?

Oh, I am unknown, even to myself
discovering
marvel.

Is this how it is with angels—so free—
though I have never seen one?

When My Body Leaves My Soul

Maybe when I am in the flames

something comes
to catch me up

like you the God I've never seen.

I don't know how to not
be
myself.

You would not dictate
how my love
severs

what makes me
think like this—

but not thinking—
I am this—

I am fire,
fire is in me—
when I touch it—

this whole book of my saying
beautiful fire, beautiful life.

To touch the fire—
do not think I am not

scared—but that happened a long time ago—
there—from the very beginning,

but enough lit in me—
already unencumbered—

maybe I am already
lighter than air. Sweet

intuition
(take) me there.

Her Last Name Is: Oblivion, Forgotten

Everyone wants me to not
say it—how it is—
come inner.

In the exquisite
humanness—asking something
beyond, beyond.

I can't believe
I would be given you

for naught.

Maybe when I get here.

Help me set each day to speak.

I am flawed, of course.
I am also beyond myself

approaching.

So this is how I see this.
No shame.

Maybe my wretchedness, maybe your goodness.

Nor Do I Have Any Other Practice

Maybe it's you
pressing at me like this.

(If I have to speak,
will you become quiet?)

Explicit

You be the voice that goes before me.

You'll have to say something.

The work of this work.

Inquiry

Why does the heart go back and forth like that?
To say I was hurt

when the elders came to speak to me?

Walking through the world in sanctuary
for these pages where I am alive.

Everything happened
so I could say this.

Locate myself

where I once walked
in my awakening.

Help me lose, use these hours—
release my limit to you.

(This really is between us.)

My mind in the book.
My own wild heart way.

The Approval

For years I tried to tell you
what the book meant to me.

It was my glimmer, my door.

When I am raw.

This is like fire—
that makes the other fire
nothing.

You see the place
to fly out of me.

You answered me
and I didn't have to understand it.

She Is Where She Loves

These walking poems
of real feelings.

Let's talk about it
whatever you are.

Maybe this is why I feel
pressing.

I am always trying
so hard.

But a little girl sings.

And I certainly don't understand death

or the afterlife
with any surety
as some speak

but I understand
beautiful book.

And my love can

answer that.

Because She Has Given Him All She Has

Your presence in the world
holds the world
for me.

The field, my field.

I need to get very quiet.

To seed this explosion in
myself.

(I would like
to be strong.)

You who do not deny me
this landscape—

how do I inhabit a place?

For They Cannot Find Her In Their Works

Maybe someone who heard
would understand this threshold.

Not to not be.

Oh, someone I am not.

Shake my head, no—
make my heart close—
to think
I am not
enough
as is.

Help me be kind
to not think that.

I am
(however they think)
merely
singularly

this voice that speaks

and then keeps speaking—till it stops.

Because No One Could Tell Me About Him

When they told me not to love anything else—
to not see the beauty and the joy—

to not take my happiness in lover, in child—

oh creature,
most magnificent

it's how I discovered
my fierceness—

and the woman who spoke

(that finally, finally)

this gentle voice came to her
that she heard

(as her own).

Into My House And Everything Surrounds

So many are living elsewhere
in their minds—

in their beings—

so much time thinking of another house
another city

another body to walk around in.

How could my voice come from this?

Right way, wrong way
messing-up way—

didn't see, didn't know—

you knew,
you know.

The thicket uncovered now—
the tree branches cleared

for a narrow opening—

like growing into myself,
growing into a life

like a relief

of myself.

Time passes and opens up

a fine statue,

a figure

ancient

coming alive—

like a live being:
reverberating ecstatic voice.

I am in another realm now.

And how could it be these pulls
and habits

(always torturous)
breaking open

dispersed.

Just standing here

speaking the voice
coming through the body, out of the body,

moving forth over the earth

into the leaves—
into the trees—

I don't even have to think anymore.

Beauty, love?:

How the leaves come in.
How the trees inhabit the land.

Three Beautiful Considerations

1.

The beauty I am trying to reach,
core center

always seeking?

2.

The voice speaks
outside of time—

outside of me

in space.

3.

To want to fly out of myself
and desire
to speak

evocation—

seems hard
at the center

but wait—

what if it's a beautiful center?

Here One Speaks

1.

All I can do is

try to be near

standing
as if a door.

And make my voice listen.
(This is the way I become the voice.)

I have to meet myself there.

2.

I am hearing it.

Oh, this Joy—

the difficult emotion,

so shunned
by mind.

Keep me from interfering with myself.

Maybe it could be a
two-part

leap to here.

3.

I know if I am in the work.

And then the voice—here—
whatever it is—

like a tree, growing freely in my garden.

Not thought

but my lover, my child

guide.

Reason And Fear And This Insatiable Will

To rest in you and believe you love me—
which is hard for me.

Because of what they have told me—
how can this be?

I am not a factory!

This is not a trite question—
the ability to love

everything I have believed in.
Everything I have forgotten.

In The High Mountain, Above The Winds

My mind closes me in.

Do you think I am idea?

I wish I knew what you thought
but that word
means judgment—so I don't think
love is

as wind moves

as energy.

I was going to say this.

If the voice is unfettered,

is the love?

How Reason Is Surprised That This Soul Has Abandoned The Virtues

Always thinking to go there—
the somewhere else was the answer—

when really
I am building this house.

And so much to see here
in time

hardly enough
to glimpse.

I feel so vulnerable
at the point of collapse—

beginning and end,
gentleness and steadiness

pushes in to voice.

I always think to go out there—
but it is in—
then here.

Maybe these pages
are the book?

Deep, Large, Supreme, And Sure

I am at such a point.
All visible light.

And the earth
filled with life.

Even the worst seemed glorious
in this exploration of feeling—

experiment upon experiment
voice calling to voice

their eyes averted to see
this cup

I raise to my mouth—

everything I said today
taken in, poured out.

Deo Gratias

What I feel when I talk to the voice,
and what the world tells me.

What I feel when I talk to the world,
and what the voice tells me.

Repose

This time I decided to rest—
my brain, quiet.

My body lifting up,

my voice, finally—
to step aside.

They say I am a *condemned woman.*

Utterly depleted—

I felt right.

How slow I go.

The Soul Is The Precious Parchment

The flames leapt up
from the trees,
parchment
burning, burning.

You heard my voice, didn't you?

The voice rising up, even
released by fire

walking through fire
the body passing through

which is more resilient—

the voice—

or this fire?

From The Ancient World

When the artifacts are found
chiseled out, cleaned up and looked at again
as things of beauty

that are not lost
(never were lost)

what do we recognize?

Sublime beauty—
exquisite human attempt?

Maybe the ringing of a bowl
sounds *blue blue*

at the same time as
light reflects

a pressing up
from a golden horse's head.

A hand touches it—
and like an intuition

it tells us it is here.
It tells us we are here.

Where no record
had ever been found

a series of tiny figurines unearth
as if to say:

I did my work, I did it right.

My First Born Daughter

Have I survived this long?

Who gives this to us?

Giving presence
to the presence?

All in the watching
was my joy.

You know.
Let this be your voice.

And I remembered these were the trees.

I was in (my) nature again.

An Addendum:

The Voice (1977)

Home—I want it, but there is
no no no where.
I want to lay my sleepy head down.
I ask myself—Can you
a mere woman change? Common woman, oh you
common common (but the voice says get up).
So I stumble, half sleeping, half speaking,
like someone drunken. I pretend
I have no legs of responsibility
(and the voice says—*You must walk,*
broken, or not. Do you hear what I am saying?
StepStepStep and another—
Your feet will walk without you; I tell you
walk or know you didn't).
So I hold myself up with my own arms,
to prove that I can stand.
They tangle around me like vine petals:
five unanswered questions, return to the dust. And
I only wanted to lie down in the black ground, held
by my blackness; it is time to be covered over
(but the voice says—*It is good for us to be here.* Again.
It is good for us to be here).

Notes

Labyrinth On My Table is indebted to Marguerite Porete's *The Mirror of Simple Souls*. Marguerite Porete was a Beguine and mystic burned at the stake in Paris in 1310 after a lengthy trial, after refusing to remove her book from circulation and recant her views. Many titles in **Labyrinth On My Table** incorporate terminology from Porete's work.

The punctuation of the epigraph from Thomas Traherne's *Centuries* is Traherne's, not typographical errors.

Acknowledgements

Grateful acknowledgment is made to the following publications in which these poems first appeared:

American Poetry Review: "In The Bed," "The Solitary Darkness," "Deep, Abiding," "For Little Bodies Bodily Thrones: For Spirits Invisible," "How She Moves Her Hand," "Everything Was Moving, And Not," "As Though I Were Awakening From A Sleep," "My Fortieth Year"

"In The Chamber Of The Voices," "In The Book Of Love, For The Not Living," "The Field," "In The Heat, The Body," "Uncreated Light," "A Chorus," "In The Open Field," "Could I Have Opened My Eyes Without You," "If I Kiss Your Forehead," "Clear Instrument," "Temple Hymn," "In The Light (The Haze) Of The Field" [cover feature]

"Marguerite Speaks," "The Voice," "The Being Toward Which She Tends," "Aperture," "A Desperate Attempt At Beauty," "Of The Work Of Love And Why She Has This Book Made," "Her Professed Religion," "More Free, And Very Free," "Nothing Other Than To See," "Like Wax From A Seal," "Labyrinth On My Table," "Ravishing Farnearness," "When My Body Leaves My Soul," "Her Last Name Is: Oblivion, Forgotten," "Nor Do I Have Any Other Practice," "Explicit," "Inquiry," "The Approval," "She Is Where She Loves," "Because She Has Given Him All She Has," "For They Cannot Find Her In Their Works," "Because No One Could Tell Me About Him," "Into My House And Everything Surrounds," "Three Beautiful Considerations," "Here One Speaks," "Reason And Fear And This Insatiable Will," "In The High Mountain, Above The Winds," "How Reason Is Surprised That This Soul Has Abandoned The Virtues," "Deep, Large, Supreme, And Sure," "Deo Gratias," "Repose," "The Soul Is The Precious Parchment," "From The Ancient World," "My First Born Daughter," "An Addendum: The Voice (1977)"

Faultline: "The House I Am In," "Looking At The Fountain In The Sun," "A Burning," "Evening Song"

Ploughshares: "Celestial Room," "The Day With Both Of Them," "Viva Vox"

"For Little Bodies Bodily Thrones: For Spirits Invisible," reprinted by *Alhambra Poetry Calendar 2008*

"How She Moves Her Hand," reprinted by *Alhambra Poetry Calendar 2009*

"If I Kiss Your Forehead," reprinted by *Alhambra Poetry Calendar 2012*

"Viva Vox," reprinted by Poetry Daily (2005) and *Alhambra Poetry Calendar 2010*

The poem "Night Watch" first appeared in the exhibition catalogue: *Habitacion 523, Jose Manuel Ballester* (Museo National Centro de Arte Reina Sofia, Madrid, Spain). It also appeared in *The American Poetry Review* as part of an essay entitled "Poetry and Mysticism."

The poem "It Is Night, In My Studio" first appeared in *The American Poetry Review* as part of an essay entitled "In the Studio."

The poem "From The Ancient World" appeared in the exhibition catalogue: *From Ancient To Modern / Archaeology And Aesthetics,* published by the Institute for the Study of the Ancient World at New York University / Princeton University Press, Princeton and Oxford.

My gratitude to William Olsen, Nancy Eimers, Kimberly Kolbe, Danielle Isaiah, Matthew Poleo, and everyone at New Issues Press and The Design Center for their kind help with the production of this book.

photo by Chi-Lin Sun Photography

Doreen Gildroy's first two books were published by the University of Chicago Press: *The Little Field of Self* in 2002 (winner of the John C. Zacharis First Book Award from *Ploughshares*) and *Human Love* in 2005. Since then, she has been working on *Trilogy*, which consists of three separate interrelated books. She has been Visiting Writer at the Vermont Studio Center, a Robert Frost Fellow at the Bread Loaf Writers' Conference, and the Visiting Poet for the MFA Program in Writing at the University of California, Irvine. Her poems have appeared in many anthologies and magazines, including *Ploughshares*, *Slate*, *TriQuarterly*, *The Virginia Quarterly Review*, and *The American Poetry Review* (which published the third book of *Trilogy* as a special supplement). She currently writes a column for *APR* on Poetry and Mysticism.

The Green Rose Prize

2017: Doreen Gildroy
Trilogy

2016: Nadine Sabra Meyer
Chrysanthemum, Chrysanthemum

2015: Bruce Cohen
Imminent Disappearances, Impossible Numbers & Panoramic X-Rays

2014: Kathleen Halme
My Multiverse

2013: Ralph Angel
Your Moon

2012: Jaswinder Bolina
Phantom Camera

2011: Corey Marks
The Radio Tree

2010: Seth Abramson
Northerners

2009: Malinda Markham
Having Cut the Sparrow's Heart

2008: Patty Seyburn
Hilarity

2007: Jon Pineda
The Translator's Diary

2006: Noah Eli Gordon
A Fiddle Pulled from the Throat of a Sparrow

2005: Joan Houlihan
The Mending Worm

2004: Hugh Seidman
Somebody Stand Up and Sing

2003: Christine Hume
Alaskaphrenia
Gretchen Mattox
Buddha Box

2002: Christopher Bursk
Ovid at Fifteen

2001: Ruth Ellen Kocher
When the Moon Knows You're Wandering

2000: Martha Rhodes
Perfect Disappearance